HAL•LEONARD INSTRUMENTAL PLAY-ALONG

TROMBONE

IRISH FAVORITES

T0085462

CONTENTS

HOW TO USE THE CD ACCOMPANIMENT:

THE CD IS PLAYABLE ON ANY CD PLAYER, AND IS ALSO ENHANCED SO MAC AND PC USERS CAN ADJUST THE RECORDING TO ANY TEMPO WITHOUT CHANGING THE PITCH.

A MELODY CUE APPEARS ON THE RIGHT CHANNEL ONLY. IF YOUR CD PLAYER HAS A BALANCE ADJUSTMENT, YOU CAN ADJUST THE VOLUME OF THE MELODY BY TURNING DOWN THE RIGHT CHANNEL.

ISBN 978-1-4234-9530-7

HAL•LEONARD® CORPORATION
7777 W. BLUEMOUND RD. P.O. BOX 13819 MILWAUKEE, WI 53213

Visit Hal Leonard Online at
www.halleonard.com

TROMBONE

❶ BELIEVE ME, IF ALL THOSE ENDEARING YOUNG CHARMS

Words and Music by
THOMAS MOORE

Moderately slow
Accordion
Play
mf
f
1.
2.
(rit. 2nd time)
mf

❷ THE BELLS OF ST. MARY'S

TROMBONE

Words by DOUGLAS FURBER
Music by A. EMMETT ADAMS

Moderately slow

Guitar
Play
mp
mf
1.
mp
2.
f

BLACK VELVET BAND

TROMBONE

Traditional

Moderately
3
Banjo
Play
mf
f
1.
2.
mf

◆4 BRENNAN ON THE MOOR

TROMBONE

Traditional

Lively
Accordion
Play
f
mf
f
1.
2.
mf

❺ COCKLES AND MUSSELS

(Molly Malone)

TROMBONE

Traditional

Moderately

Accordion
Play
mp
mf
1., 2.
3.
mp

6 THE CROPPY BOY

TROMBONE

18th Century Irish Folksong

Slowly
Flute
Play
mp
mf
1.
2.
mp

7 DANNY BOY

TROMBONE

Words by FREDERICK EDWARD WEATHERLY
Traditional Irish Folk Melody

Moderately
Piano
Play
mp legato
mf
f
1.
2
mp
2.
3

8 EASY AND SLOW

TROMBONE

Traditional

Moderately
Guitar
Play
mp
f
1.
2
2.
mp
mf
3

9 THE FOGGY DEW

TROMBONE

Traditional

Lively
Pipe
Play
f
mf
1.
2.
f
3

⑩ GREEN GROW THE RUSHES, O

TROMBONE

Traditional

Moderately
Guitar
Play
mf
f
1., 2.
3.
mf

11 THE HUMOUR IS ON ME NOW

TROMBONE

Traditional

Lively
Accordion
Play
mf
f
1.
3
mf
2.

12 I ONCE LOVED A LASS

TROMBONE

Traditional

Moderately
Guitar
Play
mf
1.
4
2.
4

13 I'LL TAKE YOU HOME AGAIN, KATHLEEN

TROMBONE

Words and Music by
THOMAS WESTENDORF

Moderately slow
Accordion

Play
mf
1.
2.

14 I'LL TELL ME MA

TROMBONE

Traditional

Lively
Pipe
Play
mf
f
1.
3
mf
2.
mf
3.
4

15 THE IRISH ROVER

TROMBONE

Traditional

Lively
Piano
Play
mf
f
mf
1.
2.

THE JOLLY BEGGARMAN

TROMBONE

Traditional

Lively
3
Accordion
Play
mf
f
1., 2.
3.
mf
2

17 THE LITTLE BEGGARMAN

TROMBONE

Traditional

Lively
Accordion
Play
mf
f
1., 2.
3.

18 MacNAMARA'S BAND

TROMBONE

Words by JOHN J. STAMFORD
Music by SHAMUS O'CONNOR

Lively March
Piccolo
Play
f
ff
1.
2.
f

19 MINSTREL BOY

TROMBONE

Traditional

Moderately

Dulcimer
Play
mf
f
mf
1.
2.

20 MY WILD IRISH ROSE

TROMBONE

Words and Music by
CHAUNCEY OLCOTT

Waltz
Piano
Play
mf legato
1.
2.

21 A NATION ONCE AGAIN

TROMBONE

Words and Music by
THOMAS DAVIS

Lively
Accordion
Play
mf
f
1.
2.
mf

22 THE OLD ORANGE FLUTE

TROMBONE

Traditional

Moderately
Flute
Play
mf
f
1., 2.
3
3.
4
mf

23 THE PATRIOT GAME

TROMBONE

Traditional

Moderately
Accordion
Play
mf legato
1., 2.
3.

24 RED IS THE ROSE

TROMBONE

Irish Folksong

Moderately
Pipe
Play
mp legato
mf
mp
1., 2.
3.
4

25 THE RISING OF THE MOON

TROMBONE

Traditional

Lively
Accordion
Play
mf
f
1., 2.
3.
mf

26 THE ROSE OF TRALEE

TROMBONE

Words by C. MORDAUNT SPENCER
Music by CHARLES W. GLOVER

Moderately
Flute
Play
mp
legato
mf
mp
1.
3
2.
rit.

27 TOO-RA-LOO-RA-LOO-RAL
(That's an Irish Lullabye)

TROMBONE

Words and Music by
JAMES R. SHANNON

Moderately
Accordion
Play
mp legato
f
1.
2.

28 THE WEARING OF THE GREEN

TROMBONE

18th Century Irish Folksong

Moderately
Accordion
Play
mf
f
mf
1., 2.
3.

29 WHEN IRISH EYES ARE SMILING

TROMBONE

Words by CHAUNCEY OLCOTT
and GEORGE GRAFF, JR.
Music by ERNEST R. BALL

Moderately
Accordion
Play
mf legato
f
1.
2.
mf

30 THE WILD COLONIAL BOY

TROMBONE

Traditional

Moderately
Accordion
Play
mf
1., 2.
3.

31 WILD ROVER

TROMBONE

Traditional

Lively
Accordion
Play
mf
f
1., 2.
3.
mf